GW00373004

TRINITY
GUILDHALL

Piano
Grade 2

Pieces & Exercises
for Trinity Guildhall examinations

2012-2014

Published by
Trinity College London
Registered Office:
89 Albert Embankment
London SE1 7TP UK

T +44 (0)20 7820 6100
F +44 (0)20 7820 6161
E music@trinityguildhall.co.uk
www.trinityguildhall.co.uk

Registered in the UK
Company no. 02683033
Charity no. 1014792

Copyright © 2011 Trinity College London

Unauthorised photocopying is illegal
No part of this publication may be copied or reproduced in any
form or by any means without the prior permission of the publisher.

Printed in England by Halstan & Co. Ltd, Amersham, Bucks.

Menuet

from *Suite quatrième pour le clavecin*

Johann Mattheson
(1681-1764)

Dynamics and articulation are editorial.
The repeats should be played in the examination.

Copyright © 2011 Trinity College London

Bourrée in D minor

Anonymous

Copyright © 2011 Trinity College London

Scherzo

from *Divertimento in F*, Hob XVI/9

Franz Joseph Haydn
(1732-1809)

Dynamics and slurs are editorial.

Copyright © 2011 Trinity College London

Andante

Daniel Steibelt
(1765-1823)

Dynamics and slurs are editorial.

Copyright © 2011 Trinity College London

Mazurka

from *Album for the Young* op. 39

Pyotr Ilyich Tchaikovsky
(1840–1893)

Copyright © 2011 Trinity College London

Gaik (Mayday Dance)

from *Melodie Ludowe*

Witold Lutosławski
(1913-1994)

Copyright © 1947 by Polskie Wydawnictwo Muzyczne – PWM Edition, Kraków, Poland.
Copyright renewed 1975 by Polskie Wydawnictwo Muzyczne – PWM Edition, Kraków.
Rights transferred to Chester Music Limited for the World (Ex Poland, Albania, Bulgaria, China, the Czech Republic and Slovakia, the former Yugoslavian States (Bosnia & Herzegovina, Croatia, Kosovo, Macedonia, Montenegro, Serbia, Slovenia), Cuba, North Korea, Vietnam, Rumania, Hungary and the former USSR).
All Rights Reserved. International Copyright Secured. Reprinted by Permission.

Petit Mystère

Simone Plé
(1897–1986)

Composer's metronome mark ♩ = 60.

Copyright © by Editions Henry Lemoine, Paris. Reproduced by permission of Editions Henry Lemoine.
All enquiries about this piece should be addressed to Editions Henry Lemoine, 27 boulevard Beaumarchais 75004 Paris, France.

www.henry-lemoine.com

Summer Swing

John DeHolt

Copyright © 2011 Trinity College London

Fanfare for the Common Cold

Herbert Chappell

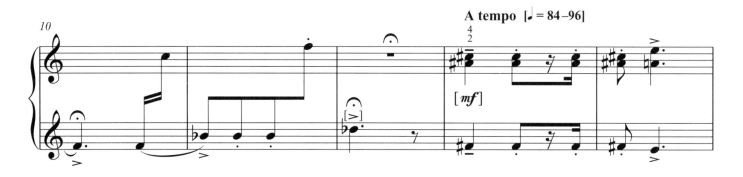

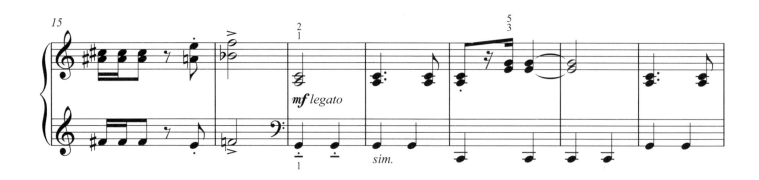

Copyright © 1995 Kevin Mayhew Ltd.
Reproduced by permission. Licence Nr. 115040/1.

(1) Two octaves higher (× = approximate pitch).

(2) The words 'Aaah! ... choo!!!' need not be spoken in the examination.

(3) Exact pitches not required − right fist/forearm cluster on black notes and left fist/forearm cluster on white notes.

- hands separately
  × 3 each hand
- Slowly, with deta

Exercises

1a. Weird Waltz – tone, balance and voicing

lighter!

Moderate Waltz tempo [♩ = 116–132]

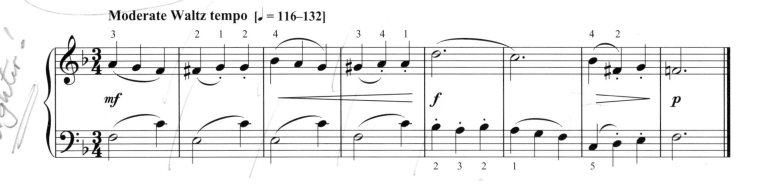

1b. The Manatee Parade – tone, balance and voicing

With a flow [♩ = 120–138]

2a. Contrasts in Touch – co-ordination

Grazioso [♩. = 54–63]

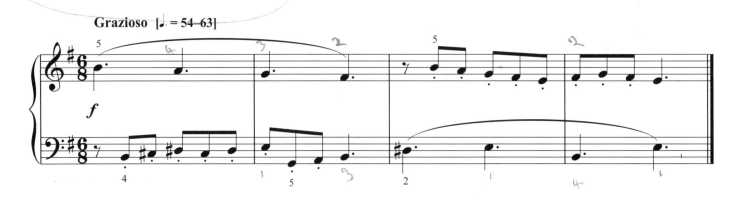

14

Copyright © 2011 Trinity College London

2b. Rag Doll – co-ordination

Lively Ragtime [♩ = 108–120]

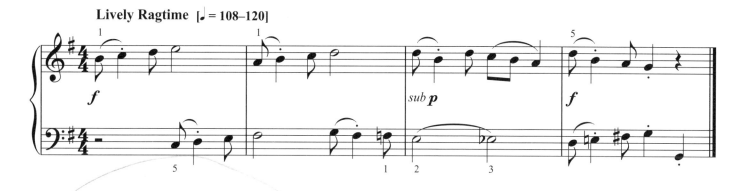

3a. Leading with the Right – finger & wrist strength and flexibility

Cantabile [♩ = 72–84]

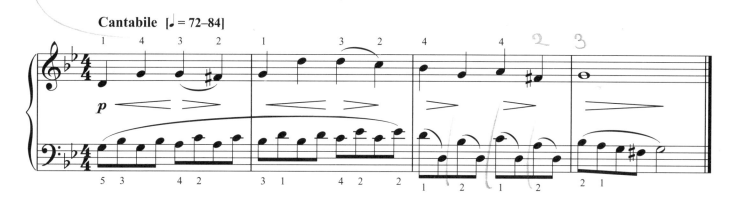

3b. Chinese Dragons – finger & wrist strength and flexibility

Inscrutably [♩ = 92–104]

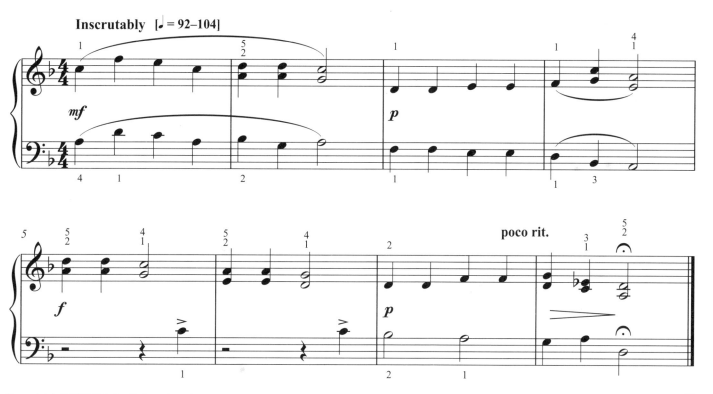

Copyright © 2011 Trinity College London